E V E R Y D A Y   H E R O E S

Everyday Heroes

J E A N N E   L A G O R I O   A N T H O N Y

©1998 by Jeanne Lagorio Anthony

Printed in the United States of America
Published by Empowerment In Action

PO Box 3064, Carlsbad, CA 92009
800-843-0165

All rights reserved.
No form of this work my be reproduced without
written permission of the publisher

Visit our Website: www.karlanthony.com/jeanne

Book Design
DesignScapes Studio™
Mapleton, OR 541-268-6937 *E-mail* design@presys.com

ISBN: 0-9633195-5-8

Library of Congress Catalog Number: 98-92878

FORWARD

by John Robbins
Author *Diet For A New America* and *Reclaiming Our Health*

Our society has a hard time with differences. We are surrounded by franchises, mass production, and assembly lines. But despite our "make a mold and stamp 'em out" attitude, it's those who are different that keep our souls alive. Like seeds sprouting through the cracks in the sidewalks, it's those who are different who are the visionaries, the dancers, the prophets, the poets, and innovators.

Whether or not you have a learning disability, and whether or not you have known anyone who has been diagnosed as having a learning disability, I'm sure there are ways, important ways, in which you are different. In whatever ways you have felt different than the norm, in whatever ways you have felt different from the herd, ***Everyday Heroes*** will help you to appreciate the strengths you have developed precisely because of the challenges you have encountered.

Those who think differently, who organize images differently, whose minds work in a unique fashion, have special challenges. As the poet E.E. Cummings once noted, it's not easy being nobody but yourself in a world that is doing it's best to make you everyone else. It's not easy being a true and authentic individual in a society that hasn't learned that the surest path to peace is to honor our differences.

Everyday Heroes is my kind of book. It helps us to understand ourselves and each other better. And Jeanne Anthony is my kind of person. Brave, authentic, wise – I'm tempted to say that if there were more people like her in our world it would be a better place. But then I catch myself, as she has helped me to do, and remember that there is only one of each of us for a reason. What we need is not more people who are copies or imitations of others, but more people who are able to honor the special qualities and talents and learning styles we each possess. *Everyday Heroes* is a fabulous book because it helps us to do just that.

In this book we meet people with learning disabilities who are pioneers, helping us to walk into a future where differences are no longer seen as grounds for shame, but as sources of understanding, acceptance, and appreciation. They help us see how to transform the pain and conflict within us into something higher, into inner strength.

DEDICATION

Mom, thank you for your pioneering spirit and seeking out the appropriate treatment for my learning challenges. The vision therapy was so very successful and just what I needed. You pursued it in spite of others' discouragement and negative beliefs about Behavioral Optometrists at that time. Also thank you for all the times you chauffeured me week after week to office visits and for helping me with my visual exercises when I was reluctant. Your patience and care have positively impacted my life forever.

Dad, a special thanks to you for helping to make treatment possible and for supporting me in all the special ways that you do.

Karl, my beloved husband, thank you for helping me to feel special rather than stupid and teaching me to laugh at my differences. I respect and cherish you!

ABOUT THE BOOK

This book provides a new loving and empowering perspective on individuals with learning disabilities, demonstrating their innate strengths and the wisdom and capacities developed in learning to cope with their challenges. From a spirit of acceptance the book serves to create greater awareness and understanding in those without such challenges, and instill hope and encouragement in those who are still struggling and suffering.

The book is based on interviews with individuals throughout the United States ranging in age from 6-58, and coming from a broad cross section of socioeconomic status.

Everyone was asked the same questions:

1) How has your learning challenge strengthened you as an individual?

2) What are some of the most vivid memories you have about being an individual with a learning difference?

3) If you had only a few moments to talk with someone struggling with a learning disability, what would you say?

It has taken me many years to appreciate my dyslexic oddities. I now realize I bring much laughter and freshness into the lives of many by just being me. How I look at situations and problem solve is very different from most people. For example phone numbers are memorized by patterns rather than numeric sequence. I can get billboards to say funny things because of seeing different words and letters. I always draft all correspondence even those to friends. I can go from thinking something costs $25,000 to realizing it actually cost $2,500. Look at all the money I saved in that moment! I'm always saving money this way.

My sister has saved every card and letter I sent to her because she finds the spelling errors endearing. In my youth these oddities would bring me to my knees in shame and embarrassment. Learning to laugh with others and to not take myself so seriously has been essential to my emotional survival as with many of the participants in this book.

ABOUT THE AUTHOR

The Author has personally struggled for many years with dyslexia. It's impact on her self-image was devastating and pervasive, but she managed to develop coping skills equal to the challenge. A turning point in Jeanne's life occurred at 13, while in a car arguing with her mother about academic performance. After what seemed to be a long time of listening to her mother talk about her potential, Jeanne blurted out in a loud voice, "I might do better if the paragraphs stopped moving around!"

Shortly thereafter vision therapy was initiated with a Behavioral Optometrist in Illinois where Jeanne was born and raised. Six short months later Jeanne could read! A whole new world of possibilities and opportunities opened up to her.

However, as a result of a late diagnosis her fundamental skills in math, reading and spelling were severely impaired. At the age of twenty, the impact of her limitations became shamefully apparent. College placement tests revealed third and sixth grade performance ability. Through persistant and tenacious efforts, Jeanne overcame her deficiencies and went on to earn a Masters degree in Social Work at the University of Illinois Chicago, Jane Adams School of Social Work. Ironically the girl who could not read at thirteen went on to write her first book thirteen years later.

Jeanne's first book, *Life Cycles*, is a guide for parents, educators and helping professionals to assist children in coping with daily change and loss. It is used by Hospices in fifty states and school districts nationwide. Anyone with a learning disability is familiar with the cycles of grief for they experience it on a daily basis. *Everyday Heroes* goes a step further, and is inspired by Jeanne's deep and sincere desire to offer hope, focus on strengths, and comfort the pain through laughter. Together let us celebrate the joys of victory, big and small. For truly, those who live with this disability are heroes every day.

CONTENTS

Unique strengths of everyday heroes 2

Memories with impact 22

Moments and wisdom to live by 42

Teachers who make a difference 60

APPENDIX

Additional Resources 66
Some Special Dyslexics 68

"IF WE DID ALL THE THINGS WE ARE CAPABLE OF DOING, WE WOULD LITERALLY ASTOUND OURSELVES."

Thomas Edison
INVENTOR

Thomas Edison was a poor student with learning disabilities and yet went on to invent the light bulb and other devices that enhanced and permanently changed the world forever.

Frustration, loneliness, embarrassment, not belonging and rage are common feelings associated with learning challenges. Moving beyond the pain to self acceptance of your own abilities is essential. Sometimes desperation is just as motivational as genius. This chapter is filled with wisdom.

STRENGTHS

How has your learning challenge strengthened you as an individual?

STRENGTHS

I can tell the story of Cinderella backwards and figured how to get paid for doing it!

Gail, 52
Humorist, California

STRENGTHS

I'm the only one that can make a 1 backwards!

Dallas, 12
Arizona

STRENGTHS

I have learned to be kind and patient with myself. I may progress slower than others but I have a strong desire to become more talented.

Marsha, 43
High school teacher, New England

STRENGTHS

I used to think I was going to quit school, now I know I'm not a quitter!

>JD, 17
>*Indiana*

S T R E N G T H S

I let others know about my learning challenges. I'm very determined, I use spell checks, calculators, time organizers, counseling and medication when prescribed. I give and get lots of hugs, this helps a lot.

> Donna, 53
> *Special Ed. Teacher, Ohio*

STRENGTHS

When I see the hope in someone else's eyes after hearing about my struggles and successes I am encouraged to never give up, whether it takes me 2 tries or 2,000. Dyslexia has helped me to be creative and to develop a sense of humor. I've learned not to sweat the small stuff and that I'm my own best material.

Gail, 52
Humorist, California

STRENGTHS

I have developed many strengths, but it has taken years of self examination to raise my self esteem and release the anger and frustration I've felt for myself and the system.

> Skip, 49
> *Masseur, Florida*

STRENGTHS

The ocean saved my life. I grew up near the beach and surfed everyday after school. If I didn't have that spiritual connection to the ocean, the effects of dyslexia might have affected me more negatively.

> Mark, 36
> *Artist, California*

STRENGTHS

My greatest strength is relentless determination!

Jeanne, 33
Therapist & Author, Illinois

STRENGTHS

Believe in yourself, it makes all the difference.

Marsha, 43
High school teacher, New England

STRENGTHS

I remember being teased a lot and really feeling inferior. In many ways it made me an over achiever. I now enjoy my success!

Barry, 29
Musician & Song Writer, Oregon

STRENGTHS

I know I can do anything as long as I try!

Erin, 12
California

STRENGTHS

I often surprise and confuse others. Sometimes while talking I say things I don't intend to because the wrong word registers in my brain. I clearly know what I want to say but the wrong word shows up. People find this humorous and often laugh. I do too when I let it. I use to beat myself up and was convinced others saw me as dumb. It's much better when I make light of it.

Jeanne, 33
Therapist & Author, Illinois

STRENGTHS

Patiently, humbly I apply myself in a steadfast manner until eventually I succeed.

Mark, 36
Artist, California

STRENGTHS

I became a class clown to offset my feelings of shame and embarrassment. I have dug deep to heal myself. Humor has helped.

Kay, 54
Health Practitioner, Texas

STRENGTHS

I learned to be resourceful, to use my fingers when counting, to ask people to repeat numbers thus verifying I have the correct number and to never leave home without my spell check or my sense of humor.

Barb, 58
Psychiatric Nurse, Colorado

STRENGTHS

Sometimes I feel like a brilliant mind trapped in a vehicle of inadequate expression. I have so many good ideas floating around in my head. I celebrate those that get out.

Mark, 36
Artist, California

STRENGTHS

As a result of my challenges I am more sensitive toward others and have developed the ability to be patient, especially with myself. I have developed a great deal of determination and know I'm not a quitter! When I get overwhelmed with paper work I take a break and then challenge myself to try harder.

Gail, 52
Humorist, Illinois

> "CHARACTER IS A BY-PRODUCT: IT IS PRODUCED IN THE GREAT MANUFACTURE OF DAILY DUTY"
>
> Woodrow Wilson, *President*

Every individual with a learning challenge knows about daily character building. Sometimes the simplest task can take hours and the smallest mistakes seem HUGE. Yet, in every experience there is opportunity and choice. It is important that we learn to keep trying, to ask for help, and most of all, to keep a sense of humor. Your attitude will influence how others respond to you.

MEMORIES

*What are some of the most vivid memories
you have about being an individual
with a learning difference?*

MEMORIES

I remember trying so hard in math class to be slow and careful with my numbers. No matter how conscientious I was or how many hours I studied, I always made dyslexic errors that ruined my score. I learned that I have other strengths and every human being has some weaknesses.

Mark, 36
Artist, California

MEMORIES

The times I have gotten lost stand out the most. One day I was on my way to a speaking engagement and I got lost. It took me 2 hours to go 10 miles. Every time someone gave me directions I became more confused. My license plate frame reads, "I've been lost before and this is what it looked like." Those kind of experiences leave a major impact. Sometimes getting lost is very scary. I have ended up in some rough neighborhoods.

Gail, 52
Humorist, Illinois

M E M O R I E S

I vividly and fondly remember making Christmas wreaths in class at school. I glued every piece on so carefully and so nicely. When I was completed I stood back and looked at it. I noticed how beautifully balanced it was. My identity had always been based on comparing myself to others. That day I came out ahead!

Mark, 36
Artist, California

MEMORIES

I felt alone, helpless, running in circles and a burden to others. When I started getting help I didn't feel so alone or helpless anymore.

Joyce, 50
Assembly Line Worker, California

MEMORIES

As a child I remember wondering why I couldn't tie my shoes like my friends. Today, I'm so proud because I can!

Kay, 54
Health Practitioner, Texas

MEMORIES

I remember one very special day after a vision therapy session when I said with excitement "Mom I'm not stupid!"

> Leslie, 16
> *California*

MEMORIES

As a child I remember looking at pages in books and seeing the words and paragraphs move around. I liked watching the patterns for a short time but was very confused by the purpose of the activity and felt left out. When we took turns reading aloud in class I would become sick to my stomach with anxiety and feel increasingly inadequate as each student read with clarity. Some students read with clarity and expression! How? How did they do this? I tried to figure out my assigned paragraph by counting the number of readers and the number of paragraphs on the page. I would practice, practice, practice, missing all of what was being read. The worst was when a good reader took on extra paragraphs and threw off my count. This worked out as a blessing when the chapter was completed before my turn! Whew! I liked it much better when my mom would read to me!

Jeanne, 33
Therapist & Author, Illinois

MEMORIES

In grade school we had spelling bees and math bees where we had to run up to the blackboard and write the answer in front of the class. I got so nervous because I couldn't do the problem that I wet my pants in front of the whole class.

Barb, 58
Psychiatric Nurse, Colorado

MEMORIES

I vividly remember getting lost going to my grandmother's house. What was so embarrassing about these moments is that it was the same house she had lived in since I was born. To make matters more humiliating I had visited her in that home monthly for 16 years. While the surroundings looked familiar I would become disoriented on which direction to take. No one made fun of me when I showed up an hour late, but I still felt stupid, like something was wrong with my brain. Memory lapses like these can come randomly and unexpectedly. I've now learned to always take directions with me. I even have a special file where I keep directions.

Jeanne, 33
Therapist & Author, Illinois

MEMORIES

It makes me mad when other people can read and I can't. I get mad at myself. Sometimes I get mad at the teacher too.

> J.D, 17
> *Indiana*

MEMORIES

In college, when other students went to bed, I'd get up and study all night.

Barb, 58
Psychiatric Nurse, Colorado

MEMORIES

While on a family vacation heading to the Grand Canyon at the age of 5 my sister and mother where teaching me to count to 10. After six hours of flash cards in the back of a station wagon, I finally had it! Only to be gravely disappointed a short while later when tested to have inaccurate recall. My mom and sister laughed in disbelief and frustration. My father on the other hand, close to numeric madness, blew up, yelling the correct order of numbers as well as some profanity! Neither volume nor repetition helped me.

Jeanne, 33
Therapist & Author, Illinois

MEMORIES

In High School I was reading a math word problem out loud and misread circumscribe and said circumcised.

> Barb, 58
> *Psychiatric Nurse, Colorado*

MEMORIES

A very embarrassing moment for me occurred at age 26, during a very important meeting. My supervisor began reading my notes from where she sat and proceeded to correct all spelling errors. Witness to this was the school principal, nurse, psychologist and several teachers with whom I worked. If I hadn't been overwhelmed and frozen by shame and embarrassment in that moment I would have leaned over and confidently said, "I prefer my personal notes to be personal." It was only later that I began to feel anger about the incident. Ironically, this supervisor was in the helping profession, and supposedly an individual trained in sensitivity and empowerment techniques. What she wasn't aware of was that phonetic spelling was more useful and practical to me than accuracy.

Jeanne, 33
Therapist & Author, Illinois

MEMORIES

I can't make change. Hours have been spent training me in this area. Finally I get it! The next day I wake up and it's gone. I've accepted that I don't make change and I've learned to trust others.

> Gail, 52
> *Humorist, Illinois*

MEMORIES

When I was in third grade my teacher told me my writing looked like chicken scratch. I wanted to burst into tears but I didn't. Instead I learned I was stupid. Now I realize it was just a stupid thing for her to say.

> Leslie, 16
> *California*

MEMORIES

My greatest childhood victory is remembered vividly and in every pore of my body. I was on an all-girl softball team, called the Bumble Bees. (By the way, several of us submitted t-shirts designs and mine won!) An early sign of dyslexic creativity. The bases were loaded, last inning and the batter hit an obvious home run. Somehow I ran fast enough, stopped in exactly the right spot and when I opened my eyes I had the ball. The crowd roared! Because of my dyslexia there was always a point in time when I could no longer track the ball and most often I missed it. This time everything lined up perfectly!

My teammates were stunned for they knew the odds of me making the play was slim to none. As a result they were overjoyed and exuberant about the catch! They all swarmed around me, put me up on their shoulders and signed the ball with encouraging words. I still have that ball.

Jeanne, 33
Therapist & Author, Illinois

"IMAGINATION IS MORE IMPORTANT THAN KNOWLEDGE. I NEVER CAME UPON MY DISCOVERIES THROUGH THE PROCESS OF RATIONAL THINKING."

Albert Einstein

One of the greatest sources of emotional pain for learning challenged individuals is not being able to succeed in the system the way others do. Healing begins when we start to see our differences as having value.

Many problems that exist in the world today are going to require creative solutions. As Einstein once said, "Problems cannot be solved at the same level of consciousness that created them." Your unique point of view can be the idea that creates postive change in the world, just like Albert Einstein.

EVERYDAY HEROES

A FEW MOMENTS

*If you had only a few moments
to talk with someone struggling
with a learning disability,
what would you say?*

JEANNE LAGORIO ANTHONY

A FEW MOMENTS

Be patient with yourself. Don't be afraid to be different. You simply have to find your learning style.

Marsha, 49
High School Teacher, New England

A FEW MOMENTS

Ask the teacher for help, don't give up and whatever you do don't fight or curse your teacher out.

JD, 17
Indiana

A FEW MOMENTS

Dyslexia is a blessing. Not only do you see things differently, creatively, but the coping skills that an individual develops makes the mind sharp and quick to react in new and different ways. I've become very verbal and creative on my feet. These skills have helped me become a good speaker/singer and song writer.

Barry, 29
Musician & Song Writer, Oregon

A FEW MOMENTS

What has it been like for you? I would listen. Then I would empathize and discuss our individual coping tactics and try to help one another.

Joyce, 50
Assembly Line Worker, California

# EVERYDAY HEROES

A FEW MOMENTS

Do not let the label of *Learning Disability* stop you from going for your dreams.

Skip, 49
Masseur, Florida

JEANNE LAGORIO ANTHONY

A FEW MOMENTS

Never give up! Instead of looking at what you do wrong, can't do or what overwhelms you, start looking at what you do well, that you enjoy, that you are strong in. Above all don't take yourself quite so seriously. Be willing to be open about your disability with other people so they can understand. Be willing to laugh at yourself and let others laugh with you. Bottom line, you're OK. Better than OK.

> Gail, 52
> *Humorist, Illinois*

A FEW MOMENTS

When you get angry and start calling yourself stupid and other hurtful names, STOP and Apologize to Yourself!

Jeanne, 33
Therapist & Author, Illinois

A FEW MOMENTS

Don't believe people who tell you that you're lazy. Lazy is a word that says look deeper. Is there confusion about what should be done or how to start?

Donna, 53
Special Ed. Teacher, Ohio

A FEW MOMENTS

I would take that child in my arms and tell them that Dyslexia is something that can be worked with and reassure them that they are bright. I would encourage them to work at their own pace and give praise for their courage.

Barb, 58
Psychiatric Nurse, Colorado

A FEW MOMENTS

The first thing I would ask is, "Do you eat sugar?" I would tell them some of the crazy negative ways sugar has affected my learning disability and definitely encourage them to not eat sugar!

Kay, 54
Health Practitioner, Texas

A FEW MOMENTS

Do you want to play with me? Do you want to eat lunch with me? Do you want me to help you with your work?

> Thomas, 6
> *California*

A FEW MOMENTS

I reverse letters too. Lots of people do that. Sometimes I scream and then ask my parents for help.

Ryan, 8
California

A FEW MOMENTS

Don't give up, there is hope. Others are struggling. I have worked hard at treatment and now I can be proud. So can you!

> Leslie, 16
> *California*

A FEW MOMENTS

Learn about other people that have conquered similar challenges.

Donna, 53
Special Ed Teacher, Ohio

A FEW MOMENTS

Dyslexia is not a disability. You can choose to view it as positive or negative. It really means you are creative and intelligent in different ways than others. Now, it is up to you to find those areas, those ways that make you stand out as someone with unique talents and ability. You are unique and talented!

> Mark, 36
> *Artist, California*

A FEW MOMENTS

I have a learning disability too. You're not a bad person.

> Frank, 29
> *Clerk, California*

EVERYDAY HEROES

> "TEACHING SHOULD BE SUCH THAT WHAT IS OFFERED IS PERCEIVED AS A VALUABLE GIFT AND NOT AS A HARD DUTY."
>
> *Albert Einstein*

Teachers are in a powerful position of permanently imprinting the minds of their students. Due to a history of failures, children with learning disabilities often see themselves as inadequate, becoming disinterested in academic performance and experiencing learning as painful. Here, we acknowledge the heart and actions of some very special teachers who helped put the joy, purpose and curiosity back into learning, positively influencing the lives of their students and through them, many countless others.

JEANNE LAGORIO ANTHONY

EVERYDAY HEROES

4

TEACHERS

Teachers who made a difference

JEANNE LAGORIO ANTHONY

TEACHERS

I remember my third grade math teacher, Mrs. Graham. I hated math, but loved going to her class because she was always so kind to me. When I went up to her desk it seemed as if time stopped. She would give me a big smile and say "What do you need, honey?" A few times she let me do my work beside her desk. I always felt smarter when next to her, as if her belief in me took away the anxiety in my body so my brain could get to work. Mrs. Graham's influence was also extra special because before her class I had Mrs. A who was six feet tall, with a stern voice. I always felt small around her and the threat of being stepped on seemed real. Her red check marks on my returned assignments was the only color I experienced in her class. Thank you Mrs. Graham for helping me feel important.

Jeanne, 33
Therapist & Author, Illinois

TEACHERS

My remedial reading teacher Mrs. Banner made reading fun! At first I dreaded going to this small class of twelve. I used to walk outside of the school building to avoid being seen walking into the "dunce class." That's the name we gave it. I can still see the pine needles on the low branches of the trees as I looked down walking to class. Mrs. Banner gave so much positive reinforcement and made reading so much fun that I began to feel good about myself and reading. So good about myself that I began walking in through the front door. I learned that I could overcome obstacles in all areas of my life.

Mark, 36
Artist, California

TEACHERS

Betty Clark was my 8th grade English and History teacher. I'm convinced that because of her I was able to have the courage to attend college. She saw the best in me, pushed me to try harder and never used red check marks. It is difficult to hide red marks from the other students. She always started with something positive. At times this must have been difficult. By the time we got to the mistakes, they weren't quite so big, weren't quite so threatening. I tried so hard for her! To this day I'm so appreciative of her sensitivity, her love and the way in which she handled me. Because of Mrs. Clark I decided I could try college.

Gail, 52
Humorist, Illinois

TEACHERS

Dare to dream is what she tells us! Mrs. Steward teaches 5th grade and is more than a teacher, she is a friend. She always notices the good in me. Dare to dream is what she tells us. I can't get this out of my head. I doodle it every where. Dare to dream! Dare to dream! When I'm struggling she kindly says, "I've seen you do better, is anything wrong?" She really cares about me. She really likes her students and because of this we look up to her and try our best.

Erin, 12
California

Additional Resources from
EMPOWERMENT IN ACTION....
to enrich yourself & others

Life Cycles: Activities for helping children cope with daily change and loss
by Jeanne Lagorio-Anthony LCSW (1991)

This wonderful book will assist you in empowering children in an easy and fun way. The innovative exercises will benefit youth by assisting them in choosing safe ways of coping with loss, increasing their awareness of community and personal resources. It helps facilitate acceptance of their own feelings and of those around them, fostering respect for themselves, others and nature.

Grades K-6 but not limited to this age group.......................$15.00

Teen Power
Co-authored by Karl Anthony and several other national teen speakers. (1996)

Encouragement for today's teens! Short inspirational & motivational stories for todays teenagers.

Grades 9 & up...$11.95

Pre-Teen Power
Co-authored by Karl Anthony and several other national youth speakers. (1997)

Encouragement for today's youth! Short, inspirational & easy to read stories.

Grades 6-8..$11.95

MUSIC WITH A POSITIVE MESSAGE

Children of the World
Issue specific songs for elementary age children.
Songs like; Don't Smoke That Cigarette & This Body is Mine. A free Karaoke version is included for personal & party fun. A masterpiece!
Double Cassette..........$20.00, *Double CD*..........$25.00

Our World
Contemporary Rock & World beat music about global cooperation and environmental responsibility...........*Cassette* $10.00

Celebrate Life
Fun, esteem building sing-a-longs for kids of all ages!
Includes favorites: Every Little Cell in my Body is Happy & I am Your Friend...*Cassette* $10.00

TO ORDER CALL OR WRITE......**1-800-843-0165**
or
Check out our website: www.karlanthony.com/jeanne

Empowerment IN ACTION

Empowerment in Action
PO Box 3064, Carlsbad, CA 92009

Some SPECIAL DYSLEXICS

Whoopi Goldberg	*Leading Actress*
Paul J Orfalea	*Businessman, Founder of Kinkos*
Bruce Jenner	*U.S. Olympic Decathlon Gold Medal Winner*
Cher	*Leading Actress, Entertainer*
Walt Disney	*Visionary & bringer of joy especially to children*
Leonardo Da Vinci	*One of the Greatest Renaissance Artist, Sculptor & Painter*
Nolan Ryan	*Athlete, Pitcher for Texas Rangers*
George Burns	*Leading Actor & Comedian*
Edward Hallowell, MD	*Author, Psychiatrist, ADD Specialist*
John Corcoran	*Real Estate Millionaire*
Albert Einstein	*A Genius, Scientist, Philosopher*
Thomas Edison	*A brilliant Inventor & Scientist*
Greg E. Legginess	*U.S. Olympic Gold Medalist*
Harry Belafonte	*Singer, Actor, Entertainer*
Jackie Stewart	*Race car driver*

EVERYDAY HEROES

Hans Christian Anderson	*Author of children's fairy tales*
Nelson Rockefeller	*Vice President of United States*
Henry Winkler	*Actor, Producer, Director, Humanitarian, "The Fonz"*
Lindsay Wagner	*Actress, Author, "The Bionic Woman"*
Gaston Caperton	*Governor of West Virginia*
Dale S. Brown	*Author, Handicapped Advocate*
David Jones	*Helicopter Pilot, Stunt Man, Pioneer in helicopter aerial photography*
Woodrow Wilson	*U.S. President*
Norla D Chee	*Award winning Poet & Author*
Nancy L Sonnabend	*Researcher, Inventor & Author*
Ellie Hawkins	*Record Breaking Rock Climber*
Tom Smothers	*Comedian & Showman*
William Simmons, MD	*Professor of Anesthesiology*
Russell White	*Athlete, Football Running Back Los Angeles Rams*
Sylvia Law	*Professor of Law & Medicine, Author*
Eric Wynalda	*Professional Soccer Player*
Edward James Olmos	*Actor & Community Activist*

EVERYDAY HEROES

John Horner	*Curator of Paleontology, Technical Advisor to Steven Spielberg for Jurassic Park & The Lost World*
Terry Bowerscok	*Entrepreneur, Motivational Speaker*
Victor Villasenor	*Award-winning Author*
Patricia Polacco	*Author and llustrator of over 30 children's books*
Bob Jimenez	*TV Anchorman*
Stephen Bacque	*Entrepreneur of the Year*
Fanny Flagg	*Actress & Screenwriter*
Ann Bancoft	*Explorer, Lecturer, Educator, 1st woman to travel across the ice to the North and South Poles*
William B Yeats	*Poet & Dramatist, Nobel Literature Prize Winner*
George Patton	*Military General*
Alexander Graham Bell	*A brilliant Inventor*
Winston Churchill	*Political Strategist*
Roger Saunders	*President of National Dyslexia Assocation*
YOU!	*What ever you choose*

* names obtained from The National Dyslexia Association, Studio City, CA and *The Gift of Dyslexia* written by Ron Davis.

JEANNE LAGORIO ANTHONY